Chantal Ar
+Theatre L

G000045313

singularity in

HOW TO ACT AROUND COPS

written by **Logan Brown** with **Matthew Benjamin**

First performed as part of the New York International Fringe Festival 2003, where it was awarded the Best Director and Best New Playwright Awards. This version premiered at the Pleasance Theatre, Edinburgh on 4 August 2004 as part of the Edinburgh Festival Fringe where it won a Scotsman Fringe First Award. Opened at Soho Theatre London on 12 October 2004.

Chantal Arts + Theatre Ltd in association with Soho Theatre Company presents

singularity in

HOW TO ACT AROUND COPS

written by **Logan Brown** with **Matthew Benjamin**

Cast in order of appearance:

Barnum	Andrew Breving
Madson	Matthew Benjamin
Cop	Chris Kipiniak
Dean	Daniel Breaker
Steph	Flora Diaz

designed and directed by Jon Schumacher
lighting design by Christoph Wagner
sound design by John Leonard and John Owens for Aurasound
original music by Marco Paguia
production manager Nick Ferguson
chief technician Nick Blount
lighting technician Ade Peterkin
graphic design Huw Jenkins at snowcreative
photography Geraint Lewis
        www.geraintlewis.com
advertising Media Junction
Press at Soho – Nancy Poole 020 7478 0142
        nancy@sohotheatre.com
On tour – Louise Chantal 07976 418 232
        louisejchantal@aol.com

The producer would like to thank: all at Soho Theatre Company especially Jon Lloyd, Nina Steiger, Mark Godfrey and Nick Ferguson; Seth Goldstein; Christopher Richardson and all at Pleasance Theatres; Suzy Somerville; James Seabright and Ben Warlow at Festival Highlights.com; Mark Christian Subias; Ed Smith at Karushi; all at the Theatre Investment Fund offices – Nick Salmon, Thelma Holt and Alexis Meach; Sean Hinds; Huw Jenkins; Robert Knight; and Jon Schumacher very, very much indeed!

The Company

Matthew Benjamin Co-writer, Madson

Has been working on COPS for two years now. Other theatre and film projects include *The Jesus Side* (Stella Adler Theatre, Los Angeles); *Aloha, Say the Pretty Girls* (CAP 21); *The Hat Left Behind* (Theatre for the New City); *Ray* (w/Jamie Foxx); *Easy* (Sundance 2004); and *The Rush Policy*. He is a native of Los Angeles.

Daniel Breaker Dean

A recent graduate of the Juilliard School. Favorite productions at Juilliard include *As You Like It*, *As Five Years Pass*, *The Love of Three Oranges*, *Hothouse*, *Riff Raff*, and *Twelfth Night*. Recent productions include *The Silent Woman*, *The Rivals*, and *A Midsummer Night's Dream* (all at the Shakespeare Theatre); *Fabulation* (Playwrights Horizons); the title role in *Pericles* (the Red Bull Theatre at the Culture Project); and Lee Blessing's *Blacksheep* (Barrington Stage). Other productions include *H M S Pinafore* (Berkshire Theatre Festival); Thea Musgrave's *A Christmas Carol* (Virginia Opera); and an appearance on *Law & Order: Criminal Intent*.

Andrew Breving Barnum

Has been with COPS since its first incarnation. Off-Broadway: Anthony in *The Karaoke Show* (Club El Flamingo). Off-Off-Broadway: Ken Urban's *Or Polaroids* and *The Death of Tintagille* (HERE Arts Center); *Long Arm of Science* with Magnetic North (Singularity's Stage '03 Festival); and Thomas Magnum in *Magnum Opus* (Stage '01). Regional: Arthur Townsend in *The Heiress* (Two River Theatre, NJ). TV: *The Jamie Kennedy Experiment*, *Guiding Light*, *All My Children*, *Strangers With Candy*.

Logan Brown writer

Writing credits include *Hogs*, *Oasis* (Hangar Theatre Lab Company) and *The Rush Policy*. Born and raised in Montana and schooled at Northwestern University, he now lives in New York.

Flora Diaz Steph

NY theatre credits include *Tooth and Claw* (Ensemble Studio Theatre), *Double Sophia* (Cherry Lane Theatre), *Women On Love* (The Culture Project), *SCAB* (Women's Expressive Theatre), *Tiny Tiny White Shorts* (SitiCompany Studio), and the New Works Now festival (Public Theatre). Regional credits include *Once Removed* (Coconut Grove Playhouse), *Fuente Ovejuna* and *The Paradise Hotel* (Court Theatre, Chicago) and a workshop production of *Crippled Sisters* (Baltimore Center Stage). She recently made an appearance on *Law and Order: Criminal Intent* and was featured with Campbell Scott in the film *Rodger Dodger*.

Chris Kipiniak Cop

Broadway: *Metamorphoses* (also Second Stage, Mark Taper Forum, Seattle Repertory, and Berkeley Repertory). Off-Broadway: *Kit Marlowe* (Public Theatre). Off-Off-Broadway: *Stalled*, *Crackwalker*, *Jane*; Regional: *W;t* and *The Odyssey* (Goodman). Film/TV: *The Secret*, *Three Flat*, *Law & Order*, *Guiding Light*, *All My Children*. Playwriting: *Stalled*, *The Big Search*, *The Nature of the Beast*. Other writing: *Nightcrawler* for Marvel Comics.

Jon Schumacher director

Founded Singularity in 1999. He was named Best Director at the 2003 New York International Fringe Festival for *How to Act Around Cops*. Company credits include *Five Frozen Embryos + The Sleepers* (2002 FringeNYC Best Overall Production), *Christmas on Mars*, *Aloha, Say the Pretty Girls*, and *Magnum Opus*, a meticulously recreated stage adaptation of *Magnum, PI*. He is also the director of The United States Project, an ongoing series of theatre biographies about real people, and directed and performed in *A Day in the Life of Clark Chipman* (1999 NY Int'l Fringe Festival), *Railways & Firework* (Manhattan Theatre Source) and *Work and Progress* (HERE Arts Center). He is a member of the Drama League Director's Project.

Singularity was founded in 1999 by Jon Schumacher, Ellen Shanman, and Jeff Tomsic, and is dedicated to creating innovative new works in theatre and film such as world premieres of David Greenspan's *Five Frozen Embryos* and Christopher Shinn's *The Sleepers* (2002 FringeNYC Best Overall Production) and original pieces by talented newcomers like Sam Forman's *Hunter for Hunter Green*.

Singularity also produces an annual festival that has served as a launching pad for some of the city's most talented young artists, as well as the acclaimed documentary series The United States Project. The latest show in the series, *United States: Work and Progress*, received the Drama League's 2002 New Directors/New Works grant and was recently published in the anthology *Plays and Playwrights 2004*. The company has also produced two short films, and recently completed post-production on Tomsic's short film, *Down Play*.

For more information, please check out our website at
www.singularitycompany.com.

Artistic Director Jon Schumacher
Director, New Media Jeff Tomsic
Director, Development Christy Meyer
Artistic Associate Ellen Shanman
Artistic Associate Greg Schmalbach

Chantal Arts +Theatre Ltd

CAT was set up in 2003 by Louise Chantal after ten years working as a producer and marketing consultant in theatre, including stints at the Soho Theatre + Writers' Centre, Pleasance Theatres and Actors Touring Company. CAT specialises in producing new writing and international companies. Recent productions include The Riot Group's First of the Firsts 2003 winner *Pugilist Specialist* (Edinburgh Festival, Soho Theatre and UK tour); *Victory at the Dirt Palace* (London season and national tour 2003); *Roadmovie* by Nick Whitfield and Wes Williams (Edinburgh Festival 2002 and UK and Eire tour 2003); *Silent Engine* by Julian Garner (with Pentabus Theatre – Fringe First winner Edinburgh Festival 2002 and UK tour) and a British Council tour in Israel of Theatre de l'Ange Fou's *The Government Inspector*.

The Riot Group's PUGILIST SPECIALIST opened at 59e59 Theatre off-Broadway in New York City in September 2004. Productions this year include Will Eno's Fringe First and Herald Angel Awards winner *Thom Pain (based on nothing)* with *The Stage* Best Actor Award winner James Urbaniak (co-produced with Soho Theatre Company at the Edinburgh Festival 2004 and London). *Thom Pain* will open in New York in 2005. Louise is also Associate Producer at Pentabus Theatre and will tour Bryony Lavery's epic production of *Precious Bane* internationally in 2005.

The company undertakes a variety of contracts and consultancies ranging from full-scale theatre productions to general management, tour booking and publicity.

www.chantalarts.co.uk, 3rd Floor, 118 Wardour Street, London W1V 3LA
email: louisejchantal@aol.com
tele: 020 7439 1175   fax: 020 7434 0932

The Theatre Investment Fund

How to Act Around Cops was produced with the assistance of a New Producer's Bursary from the Theatre Investment Fund, which is a UK registered charity (no. 271349). The TIF assists new producers and invests in productions throughout the UK. The producer would like to extend her thanks to everyone involved in the TIF, especially the following who generously support new work:

The Society of London Theatre

The Arts Council of England

The Mackintosh Foundation

Clear Channel Entertainment UK

The Equity Trust Fund

How To Act Around Cops will tour the UK from January 2005.
For full details please check www.chantalarts.co.uk.

● soho
● theatre company

Bars and Restaurant

Café Lazeez brasserie serves Indian-fusion dishes until 12pm. Late bar open until 1am. The Terrace Bar serves a range of soft and alcoholic drinks.

Email information list

For regular programme updates and offers, join our free email information list by emailing box@sohotheatre.com or visiting www.sohotheatre.com/mailing.

If you would like to make any comments about any of the productions seen at Soho Theatre, visit our chatroom at www.sohotheatre.com

Hiring the theatre

Soho Theatre has a range of rooms and spaces for hire. Please contact the theatre managers on 020 7287 5060, email hires@sohotheatre.com or go to www.sohotheatre.com for further details.

● soho
● theatre company

Artistic Director: Abigail Morris
Acting Artistic Director: Jonathan Lloyd
Assistant to Artistic Director: Nadine Hoare
Administrative Producer: Mark Godfrey
Assistant to Administrative Producer: Tim Whitehead
Writers' Centre Director: Nina Steiger
Literary Officer: David Lane
Education and Workshop Officer: Suzanne Gorman
Casting Director: Ginny Schiller
Marketing and Development Director: Zoe Reed
Development Manager: Gayle Rogers
Marketing Officer: Jenni Wardle
Marketing and Development Assistant: Kelly Duffy
Press Officer: Nancy Poole (020 7478 0142)
General Manager: Catherine Thornborrow
Front of House and Building Manager: Julia Christie
Financial Controller: Kevin Dunn
Book Keeper: Elva Tehan
Box Office Manager: Kate Truefitt
Deputy Box Office Manager: Steve Lock
Box Office Assistant: Janice Draper, Paula Henstock, Leah Read, Will Sherriff Hammond and Natalie Worrall.
Duty Managers : Mike Owen, Peter Youthed and Miranda Yates

Front of House staff: Rachel Bavidge, Louise Beere, Sharon Degen, Matthew Halpin, Siobhan Hyams, Colin Goodwin, Minho Kwon, Iain Marshall, Katherine Smith, Rachel Southern and Maya Symeou.
Production Manager: Nick Ferguson
Chief Technician: Nick Blount
Chief LX: Christoph Wagner
Lighting Technician: Ade Peterkin

Board of Directors (*) and Members of the Company:

Nicholas Allott*
David Aukin – chair*
Lisa Bryer
Tony Buckley
Sophie Clarke-Jervoise*
Cllr Robert Davis
Barbara Follett MP*
Norma Heyman*
Bruce Hyman
Lynne Kirwin
Tony Marchant

Michael Naughton*
David Pelham*
Michael Pennington
Sue Robertson*
Philippe Sands
Eric H Senat*
Meera Syal
Marc Vlessing*
Zoë Wanamaker
Sir Douglas Wass
Richard Wilson OBE
Roger Wingate*

Honorary Patrons

Bob Hoskins *president*
Peter Brook CBE
Simon Callow
Sir Richard Eyre

Development Committee

Bruce Hyman – *chair*
Nicholas Allott
David Aukin
Don Black OBE
David Day
Catherine Fehler
Nigel Gee
Madeleine Hamel
Marie Helvin
Norma Heyman
Cathy Ingram

Carol Jackson
Roger Jospé
Lise Mayer
Patricia McGowan
Michael Naughton
Jane O'Donald
Marc Sands
Philippe Sands
Barbara Stone
Des Violaris
Richard Wilson OBE
Jeremy Zimmerman

THE SOHO THEATRE DEVELOPMENT CAMPAIGN

Soho Theatre Company receives core funding from Arts Council England, London and Westminster City Council. In order to provide as diverse a programme as possible and expand our audience development and outreach work, we rely upon additional support from trusts, foundations, individuals and businesses.

All of our major sponsors share a common commitment to developing new areas of activity and encouraging creative partnerships between business and the arts.

We are immensely grateful for the invaluable support from our sponsors and donors and wish to thank them for their continued commitment.

Soho Theatre Company has launched a new Friends Scheme to support its work in developing new writers and reaching new audiences. To find out how to become a Friend of Soho Theatre and what you will receive in return, contact the development department on 020 7478 0111, email development@sohotheatre.com or visit www.sohotheatre.com

Sponsors: Angels Costumiers, Arts & Business, Bloomberg, Getty Images, TBWA\GGT

Major Supporters: Calouste Gulbenkian Foundation · The Foyle Foundation · Roger Jospé · The Regent Street Association · The Garfield Weston Foundation · The Harold Hyam Wingate Foundation · Roger Wingate

Education Patrons: Tony and Rita Gallagher · Nigel Gee · Jack and Linda Keenan

Trusts and Foundations: Anon · Sidney and Elizabeth Corob Charitable Trust · Delfont Foundation · The Follett Trust · JG Hogg Charitable Trust · Hyde Park Place Estate Charity · John Lewis, Oxford Street · The Mackintosh Foundation · The Royal Victoria Hall Foundation · The St James's Trust · The Kobler Trust · The Edward Lois Siess Charitable Trust · The Hazel Wood Charitable Trust

Dear Friends: Anonymous · Jill and Michael Barrington · Jos Chambers · Madeleine Hamel · Robert Paddick, Commonwealth Partners Ltd. · SoFie and Le'le' · Richard and Diana Toeman · Jan and Michael Topham

Friends: Thank you also to the many Soho Friends we are unable to list here. For a full list of our patrons, please visit www.sohotheatre.com

Registered Charity: 267234

Logan Brown with Matthew Benjamin

HOW TO ACT AROUND COPS

First published in 2004 by Oberon Books Ltd.
(incorporating Absolute Classics)
521 Caledonian Road, London N7 9RH
Tel: 020 7607 3637 / Fax: 020 7607 3629
e-mail: oberon.books@btinternet.com
www.oberonbooks.com

A catalogue record for this book is available from the British Library.

ISBN: 1 84002 497 6

Printed in Great Britain by Antony Rowe Ltd, Chippenham.

Characters

MADSON

BARNUM

DEAN

STEPH

COP

Regarding Lighting:

Light comes only from justified sources.
Blackness is true blackness, not 'stage night' lighting

Regarding Set:

Car may be constructed with four chairs behind a black
rectangular box representing seats and a dash.

Regarding Pacing:

Fast between the pauses.

ACT ONE

Highway at night. Blackness. Tires hum on asphalt. Two headlights appear (DSC). Inside, two men are lit by dashlight: the driver, MADSON, and another man, BARNUM, sitting shotgun. Pause.

BARNUM: Watch out that's a cop.

MADSON: Oh shit.

> *MADSON brakes.*

BARNUM: Don't stop.

MADSON: Are you sure?

BARNUM: Keep going.

MADSON: Should I turn?

BARNUM: Go straight.

MADSON: It's okay?

BARNUM: It's alright.

> *Beat.*

MADSON: Shit, they turned around.

> *Headlights of a second car silhouettes both figures. The twin beams reflect in MADSON's rearview mirror, casting a small horizontal rectangle across his eyes.*

> It's a cop?

BARNUM: It looked like a cop.

MADSON: Look at the headlights.

BARNUM: I am.

MADSON: Are they square headlights?

BARNUM: They're pretty square.

MADSON: So it's a cop?

BARNUM: I don't know.

MADSON: Well are they cop headlights?

BARNUM: Well do you know cop headlights? Are these them? How the fuck do I know what kind of square they are? They look pretty square. Are they square like cops, like fucking pigs? I don't know man, I'm not some fucking cop geek.

Pause.

MADSON: Are those lights on top?

BARNUM: I can't tell.

MADSON: Those are lights.

BARNUM: I can't even see that far.

MADSON: No I can see them. They're lights.

BARNUM: Okay.

MADSON: So fuck.

BARNUM: So it's a cop.

MADSON: So hide the shit.

Beat.

BARNUM: What shit?

MADSON: The fucking shit, dude.

BARNUM: How fast are you driving?

MADSON: Think we can outrun them?

BARNUM: I think it's a bad idea to fuck with cops.

MADSON: Oh man, I can't deal with cops.

BARNUM: There go the lights.

A siren begins: the horizontal bar flashes red and blue across MADSON's eyes.

MADSON: Oh shit. Oh no.

BARNUM: Breathe normally or you'll sweat.

MADSON: Would you just hide the shit man? I feel there could be shit here, that could, you know, somehow turn out, like, bad shit, you know, bad shit.

BARNUM: What shit?

MADSON: Bad shit.

BARNUM: Where?

MADSON: Look around.

BARNUM: Shouldn't you pull over?

MADSON: After you hide the fucking shit.

BARNUM: I just don't know what the fuck you're talking about.

MADSON: I'm talking about just look around man, and anything resembling alcohol, drugs, weapons or fucking bombs man, fucking bombs bombs bombs man, bombs. There's no telling what they will construe if we give them the slightest opportunity.

Beat.

My head is pounding. Is that my head?

BARNUM: Pull over.

MADSON: I'm not pulling over until you look around and hide whatever it is they're going to try to arrest us for.

BARNUM: Okay, Jesus man okay.

Siren continues as BARNUM looks in backseat.

BARNUM: I don't see anything.

MADSON: Okay okay, then I'm pulling over.

BARNUM: We'll be lucky if we don't get shot.

Car slows onto shoulder.

Behind, the siren stops, but red and blue lights continue flashing in MADSON's eyes.

Engine cuts off.

MADSON: What did we do?

BARNUM: Let's stop and think rationally.

MADSON: We're in the shit, dude.

BARNUM: I'm good in these kinds of situations.

MADSON: Should we just bolt?

BARNUM: They've got our license plate.

MADSON: There's no shit right?

BARNUM: No.

MADSON: This fucking pounding.

BARNUM: Listen man, these guys are cops. They're here for society, to protect and serve citizens. We are citizens, so far as I know, we should be okay.

MADSON: Is your head – ?

BARNUM: Listen, calmness, ease, ease, thinking, logic, rational thought.

Pause.

MADSON: Okay. Okay.

BARNUM: Oh fuck, she must've left her purse.

MADSON: Who?

BARNUM: Guess.

MADSON: No.

BARNUM: Yes.

MADSON: We've got her fucking purse?

BARNUM: Yes.

MADSON: Oh fuck.

>*Beat.*

>I don't even know her name.

BARNUM: Right, me neither.

MADSON: Wait, who was she?

BARNUM: Shut up dude.

MADSON: One of your women?

BARNUM: Mine?

>*Beat.*

MADSON: I know her?

BARNUM: Just shut up.

MADSON: Who is she?

>*Beat.*

>Dude.

BARNUM: What?

MADSON: Well, where did she go?

>*MADSON and BARNUM stare at each other.*

BARNUM: We should focus on the problem.

MADSON: The problem?

BARNUM: The purse.

MADSON: Okay, what're we gonna do with it?

BARNUM: I'll stow it under the seat.

MADSON: They'll see you.

BARNUM: We can't just leave it out.

MADSON: I can't even think, can you think? Does your head – ?

BARNUM: Yes.

Beat.

MADSON: What could it be – aneurism?

BARNUM: Brain aneurism?

MADSON: What are the symptoms?

BARNUM: Pain, followed by death.

Beat.

MADSON: Why're they taking so long?

BARNUM: I'm going to look in the purse. I'll be sly about it.

BARNUM reaches back.

MADSON restrains him.

MADSON: I swear to God man, don't fucking do anything.

BARNUM: I'm here to help you man. We both agree they want to fuck us. We don't know what's in the purse. What if they look in the purse? What if there's some shit in there?

BARNUM retrieves purse.

See how easy that was?

MADSON: Look in there for aspirin.

BARNUM: Oh fuck.

MADSON: What's in there?

BARNUM: Some coke and a gun.

MADSON: Oh god – oh my god.

BARNUM: Stop being a pussy. I'm just fucking with you.

MADSON: What's in there then?

BARNUM looks in purse.

BARNUM: Some coke and a gun.

MADSON: Fucking coke and a gun?

BARNUM: See?

BARNUM tilts purse.

MADSON peers inside.

MADSON: You're gonna have to eat that.

BARNUM: What the fuck is she doing with all this shit?

BARNUM removes a small plastic baggie from purse.

MADSON: Have you ever eaten coke?

BARNUM: No.

MADSON: Sniffed or injected?

BARNUM: No.

MADSON: How much is there?

BARNUM: I don't know.

MADSON: Enough to overdose?

BARNUM: I don't fucking know.

MADSON: Should we risk it?

BARNUM: It looks like a lot of coke.

MADSON: Don't eat it then, if you're gonna overdose.

BARNUM: I'll eat it.

BARNUM eats bag contents.

MADSON: I don't know about this, man.

BARNUM: Okay, I ate the coke.

MADSON: What about the gun?

BARNUM: Jesus dude, one thing at a time.

MADSON: My fucking head, dude. I'm gonna tell them my brain is dripping out of my brainpan, and it's affecting my judgment.

BARNUM: You should fucking talk.

MADSON: I gotta lay down or something in the back seat, just for a second.

BARNUM: Don't do that.

MADSON: Why?

BARNUM: Dude, they're cops, they'll shoot you.

MADSON: Fuck.

BARNUM: Shoot you dude.

MADSON: You're totally right.

Pause.

They're taking so fucking long.

BARNUM: So we'll keep the gun in the purse?

MADSON: They'll see the purse.

BARNUM: I'll keep it.

MADSON: What if they search you?

BARNUM: So I'll put it in the purse.

MADSON: What are we going to do with it?

BARNUM: It's not fitting under my seat.

MADSON: Why not?

BARNUM: It's too big.

MADSON: On the floor in the back.

BARNUM: I'm feeling the coke.

MADSON: It's fine no problem. The first thing we say is –
we say some chick, who we don't really know, left her
purse in our car and we don't know what's in there. We
just want to say that. That's all, no more and make
nothing more of it, or us, walk along officers, or stay,
either way, we're cool, if you're cool, if you're not cool,
we're not cool until you're cool. Either way, we're sober.

Beat.

We can't tell them that. They find the gun and don't
believe us. We have to tell them about the gun. We have
to tell them. We have to be honest, yep, give me the gun,
honesty is the key here, give me the gun, honestly, I'll
give it to them.

BARNUM: They'll shoot you.

MADSON: Right.

BARNUM: Fucking shoot you dude.

Beat.

23

MADSON: Okay, that's not in my head.

BARNUM: I'm on a lot of coke.

MADSON: I can't talk to the cops. It's just too much. I can't hear anything. I can't hear myself. What did I just say? I don't know. It's this fucking pounding.

BARNUM: Yep, so you're fucked. You're gonna get shot.

MADSON: What are they talking about in there?

BARNUM: There's only one in there.

One thump from trunk.

MADSON: One?

BARNUM: One.

Two thumps from trunk.

MADSON: I mean you're hearing this right?

BARNUM: You're hearing voices?

MADSON: Shut the fuck up dude, you can't hear that?

BARNUM: What the fuck are you talking about?

Three thumps from trunk.

MADSON: Is that the girl?

BARNUM: The girl?

MADSON: Is that the purse girl?

BARNUM: Is what the purse girl?

Beat.

Two thumps from trunk.

I think the coke was a bad idea.

MADSON: Something's in there.

BARNUM: Hahaha. Hey you in there –

Beat.

Be quiet.

MADSON: Hahaha.

BARNUM: Hahaha.

Car door opens.

Boots step out onto gravel.

Car door shuts.

Here he comes.

MADSON: Have I been drinking?

A flashlight clicks on behind BARNUM and MADSON.

Footsteps crunch toward them as the flashlight nears.

BARNUM: I hope he doesn't see the fucking purse.

MADSON: Someone's in the fucking trunk.

BARNUM: Hahaha.

MADSON: Hahaha.

BARNUM: No speaking.

Beat.

MADSON: Seriously, did I have a beer?

BARNUM: He's right there.

MADSON: Did I?

Knuckles rap on MADSON's window three times.

Flashlight shines into BARNUM and MADSON's faces.

I think I had a beer.

BARNUM: Roll down the window.

MADSON: Can you smell it on my breath?

BARNUM: I can't smell anything.

MADSON: Come on, man.

BARNUM: Roll down the window.

MADSON rolls down window.

COP: Excuse me.

MADSON: Officer – sir. We were –

COP: Is everything alright?

BARNUM: What do you mean?

MADSON: We were, momentarily startled back there – I thought I saw something in the middle of the road. An animal. I saw it with such clarity, like it was in slow motion. It was – uh deer, running into the road, I swerved, almost ran into you, uh, and was like whoa.

COP: Have you boys been drinking any alcohol tonight?

MADSON: No sir.

COP: Why didn't you stop?

BARNUM: It was hard to find a good place to pull over.

COP: Right, okay, give me your –

MADSON: License I bet right?

COP: License and registration, please.

MADSON: And registration, right, of course.

BARNUM: Haha, that's really bright.

MADSON: Can I ask you why you pulled us over tonight, officer?

COP: Do you know how fast you were going?

MADSON: The exact speed?

Beat.

Well approximately –

BARNUM: 67.

MADSON: 80?

BARNUM: 68.

MADSON: Well possibly 75.

BARNUM: 69.

MADSON: Probably around 72 then.

BARNUM: It felt like 67, 68.

MADSON: We'll go with felt like 70, probably…a little more, maybe.

BARNUM: A little at most.

COP: 62.

Pause.

BARNUM: A good speed.

MADSON: What is the uh speed limit around here?

BARNUM: Was there a sign?

COP: Get your license and registration out for me.

MADSON reaches over BARNUM and opens glove box.

COP shines flashlight in backseat.

BARNUM: Everything okay officer?

COP: Is that your purse, son?

BARNUM: Purse?

COP: The purse there.

BARNUM: Oh, there's a purse.

COP: Right.

BARNUM: Not mine.

MADSON: Or mine.

COP: Whose is it?

MADSON: I think it's a girl's.

COP: Right.

BARNUM: Just some girl we kind of know.

MADSON: Not that well.

BARNUM: She must have left it there. We don't even know what's inside.

COP: Let's see it.

BARNUM: Officer, the thing is, there's a perfectly logical explanation for everything here, including our strange behavior and, and we are eager to clarify everything. Frankly, I'm happy you're checking out the situation. I know I would if I were you.

MADSON: His father's a policeman.

COP: Really?

BARNUM: Yea, not like I'm asking for leniency or anything, but yea, my dad's a cop. You probably know him – Officer Barnum?

COP: I'm fairly new so –

BARNUM: Fairly?

COP: Yes, so I don't know everyone yet.

BARNUM: Oh really so…you're not supposed to patrol alone then are you?

Beat.

COP: Hand me the purse.

BARNUM turns to retrieve purse.

Two thumps from trunk.

MADSON and BARNUM look at COP. COP looks back at them.

Beat.

The purse.

BARNUM: Right.

MADSON pulls a wad of papers from glove box.

MADSON: Anyway, here's my license, and the registration is in here…somewhere…I can never find it. Is this it? No, I can't tell. Can you see it here?

MADSON gives COP wad of papers.

I can hold that for you.

MADSON takes flashlight.

COP: Keep your hands inside the car.

MADSON: Sorry.

MADSON drops flashlight.

Let me get that for you.

MADSON opens door.

COP backs up two steps and draws his gun.

COP: Freeze.

BARNUM: Don't shoot us.

MADSON: We're not criminals.

COP: Put your hands on the dash.

BARNUM and MADSON place hands on dash.

COP retrieves flashlight, clamps it in his armpit, still covering BARNUM and MADSON with his gun, and kicks the door closed.

BARNUM: Don't shoot us.

COP places wad of paper on hood.

With his free hand, he opens rear car door and extracts purse.

MADSON: Actually officer, be careful because there's a gun in there.

BARNUM: He's kidding.

COP: There's a gun in the purse?

MADSON: Hahaha, well…

COP searches purse.

BARNUM: What he's referring to is a widely held suspicion that this girl, the girl whose purse this is, often carries a gun. Not because of anything illegal, but because, because she was once attacked, raped actually sir, and now everyone says she carries a gun but we don't know we haven't looked you know?

COP: Where's the gun?

BARNUM: We've never actually seen the gun – it's all supposition.

COP loops purse over his shoulder, retrieves wad of paper

*from hood, searches through it, extracts registration and stuffs
the remainder of wad in purse.*

MADSON: Sorry everything is so confused. I get headaches
and amnesia from my epileptic seizures.

COP: Right, okay, step out of the vehicle please.

Pause.

MADSON: I'm serious, I'm an epileptic.

COP: Step out of the vehicle.

MADSON: Just – know that.

COP: Move.

MADSON: Okay.

MADSON opens door.

Sneakers crunch on gravel.

COP places MADSON's hands behind his head.

COP: Spread your legs.

MADSON spreads his legs.

Relax, I'm going to search you now.

COP searches MADSON.

What's this?

A motel key dangles in the light.

MADSON: Oh well, it looks like…a key?

COP: Obviously.

MADSON: Weird man.

COP: A motel key.

MADSON: Oh yea, I stayed in a motel last night. I must not've returned it.

COP: You don't live around here?

MADSON: I do, just for uh, kind of vacation.

COP: Uh-huh. Stay calm. If you're obeying the law you have nothing to worry about. I'm going to search you one more time.

COP pockets key and searches MADSON again.

Relax. I'll talk you through it. Chest, waist, belly, hips, crotch, inner thigh, crotch –

MADSON: Twice?

COP: Twice – what's this?

A leather gag dangles in the light.

It's a little rubber ball.

MADSON: Weird.

COP: One?

MADSON: One.

BARNUM: One.

COP: …attached to a strap.

MADSON: It's for…

BARNUM: It's a mouth gag. In fact, now that this object has come up, I'd like a chance to explain it, and I think, you'll realize it's the same explanation as to why we were acting so strangely before, the purse-slash-gun thing and uh speeding – or not, depending on what the speed limit actually is around here.

MADSON: To get me to the hospital. Epileptic seizures. I forget what I'm doing.

COP: You have epileptic seizures?

BARNUM: That's why the gag. We had a seizure scare, he thought he was choking and we couldn't find that gag thing and wouldn't you know it was in his pocket but the danger is he'll swallow his tongue.

COP: Right.

MADSON: I'm doing okay now.

BARNUM: And that's why we noticed you.

MADSON: And I have a terrible headache officer.

COP guides MADSON into the car.

COP: Okay, take it easy, Mr Madson. Keep your hands on the dash.

MADSON: Uh is that really necessary? I mean am I under arrest? I mean I haven't done anything wrong, but I'm nervous.

COP: Why?

MADSON: Just because man I'm, I'm...deathly afraid of cops, officer, it's like a phobia.

Beat.

COP: Okay, you just sit tight, I'll be right back. Don't move.

Crunching of gravel.

Flashlight moves away.

Pause.

MADSON: Who the fuck is Madson dude?

BARNUM: That's you.

MADSON: Oh Madson.

BARNUM: Like your name.

Beat.

MADSON: This is fucked up.

BARNUM: It isn't good.

MADSON: Or is it cool?

BARNUM: Or is he calling for backup?

MADSON: He didn't talk much.

BARNUM: Because you freaked him out.

MADSON: Maybe we should bolt?

BARNUM: Or shoot him with the gun.

Beat.

What was all that shit about epilepsy?

MADSON: What do you mean?

BARNUM: Amnesia?

Beat.

MADSON: I can't remember anything.

BARNUM: Really?

MADSON: Like right now literally I can't remember your name.

BARNUM: You don't know me?

MADSON: I can't remember your name.

Three thumps from trunk.

BARNUM: What do you remember?

MADSON: Like what?

BARNUM: You say you don't remember my name but you didn't say you don't know me. I'm asking how much do you remember?

MADSON: Well I'm saying should I remember something? Is there something I should remember?

Beat.

BARNUM: Think dude. What do you remember about tonight?

MADSON: The cop thing.

BARNUM: No. Before that.

MADSON: …nothing.

BARNUM: Nothing?

Beat.

MADSON: It's like –

BARNUM: What was that gag?

MADSON: Yea, that's weird.

Beat.

BARNUM: What the fuck was that gag, dude?

MADSON: I really honestly do not remember.

Beat.

BARNUM: Well look for something to jog your memory.

MADSON: Like what?

BARNUM: A ring, a scar, bruises, stains…

MADSON: Uh –

BARNUM: Yea, look in your pocket.

MADSON: A stain.

BARNUM: A stain?

MADSON: On my pants.

Beat.

BARNUM: What color is it?

MADSON: Hard to tell.

BARNUM: Wet or dry?

MADSON: In between.

BARNUM: Recently dry?

MADSON: Moist.

BARNUM: Not white?

MADSON: No.

BARNUM: Red?

MADSON: Could be red.

BARNUM: Smell it.

MADSON: I can't bend that far. You smell it.

BARNUM: I'm not gonna smell it.

MADSON: Then why did you ask me to smell it?

BARNUM: Dude, look at your knuckles.

Beat.

MADSON: Wow.

BARNUM: Okay, okay.

MADSON: Oh my fucking god.

BARNUM: Listen, forget about it, forward thinking.

Crunching steps toward them.

Flashlight silhouettes BARNUM and MADSON.

MADSON: Okay, forward thinking, here's the plan: he doesn't find the gun, we remain normal, forget about the trunk, which should be easy because I can't even remember my fucking name, and maybe he'll let us go. Unless we can't keep it together, unless the headaches overcome us he gets suspicious and we get shot or die from a fucking aneurism.

BARNUM: Don't let him see your knuckles.

MADSON: And what the fuck happened to my knuckles man?

BARNUM: Oh come on.

MADSON: No man I don't know.

BARNUM: You know man you obviously know.

MADSON: I don't know, I really don't know man… I don't.

BARNUM: Okay man whatever here he comes.

MADSON: Wait hold on where's the gun?

BARNUM: I've got it. So you should take it.

MADSON: Why?

BARNUM: Because he already searched you.

MADSON: Very bad idea.

BARNUM: I'm serious, here take it.

MADSON: I can't pull it off.

BARNUM: Take it.

MADSON: I'll choke.

BARNUM: Take it.

BARNUM stuffs gun in MADSON's pants.

COP shines flashlight on MADSON.

COP: What's going on here?

MADSON: Hello officer, listen, I just want to be completely honest – we have to tell you something, the truth, that might possibly be…misconstrued…

COP: What were you just doing?

BARNUM: Trying to remember, but we can't. We can't remember anything. We don't even know who we are.

COP: Step out of the vehicle please.

BARNUM: Me?

COP: Step out of the vehicle.

BARNUM: No problem.

BARNUM opens door.

Sneakers crunch on gravel.

COP searches BARNUM.

COP: Are you telling me you both have epileptic amnesia?

MADSON: I have epileptic amnesia, so I can't remember who he is.

COP: And you?

BARNUM: Well, officer, I sure am disoriented – I don't think I have epileptic amnesia, but I'm confused – and excited. I think we might have been drugged.

COP: So he's drugged up and an epileptic amnesiac, but you're just drugged up?

BARNUM: Right.

COP: Are you sure you're not an epileptic amnesiac too? Maybe you're brothers. Can I see your identification please?

BARNUM: Can I see your identification while you're at it?

COP: Hand me your ID.

BARNUM: It's my legal right to see yours first.

COP forces BARNUM down, holds the badge above him and shines the flashlight in his eyes.

COP: See that?

BARNUM: Oh yea. You're a cop.

COP: Hand me your identification.

BARNUM hands the cop his license.

BARNUM: See that? Barnum. Did you check on that? Call my dad. He'll straighten this out.

COP: Okay, so you're Barnum, but he's Madson, so you're not brothers.

BARNUM: No, I never said we were brothers.

COP: What's your relationship then?

BARNUM: We're old friends.

COP: Do you know him?

MADSON: I have amnesia.

COP: Well that explains everything.

MADSON: I am an epileptic amnesiac.

COP: So you don't know who he is?

MADSON: Not right now.

COP: Oh come on.

MADSON: I have amnesia, it's like that – I forget everything for about ten minutes –

COP: Only ten?

MADSON: – And then I start remembering things. It's really fucking scary man. Things are starting to clear up. I think I know him. I think he knows me.

COP: Wait, now you know him?

BARNUM: Of course we know each other.

MADSON: He knows me, peripherally, he knows I get amnesia –

BARNUM: You don't get amnesia.

MADSON: Yes I do, but now I remember – he's done something bad officer – he, he's raped a girl, she's in the trunk.

BARNUM: He's got a gun.

MADSON: No.

COP steps back and draws his gun.

COP: Freeze.

MADSON: He's lying.

BARNUM: It's in his pants.

COP: Both of you freeze.

MADSON: Okay, okay, take it away officer. It's in my pants.

COP covers MADSON and BARNUM alternately, moving to the driver's side window.

COP: Take it easy, I'm just going to take the gun.

COP removes the gun.

MADSON: He planted it on me.

BARNUM: He's setting me up.

One thump from trunk.

MADSON looks back at trunk.

MADSON: He kidnaps this girl, throws her in the trunk, he knocks me out, that explains the headache, bloodies up my knuckles-see? The strange stain on my pants. Is there blood in my hair? He "found" this gun casually in the course of natural conversation and planted it on me and now I look guilty.

Two thumps from trunk.

Stop pounding back there.

COP: What pounding?

MADSON: You can't hear that? She's fucking dying.

Three thumps from trunk.

COP: Holy shit – what is that?

MADSON: I just told you she's in the fucking trunk.

COP moves to trunk.

MADSON starts to convulse.

BARNUM: That's not possible.

COP: Open the trunk.

Sustained thumping from trunk begins.

MADSON: I'm going into seizure.

MADSON doubles over.

BARNUM: He's going into seizure. Where's the gag?

COP: Open the trunk.

BARNUM: Honest officer, look at his mouth.

COP: What is that?

BARNUM: It's foam.

COP pulls MADSON up.

Foam bubbles from MADSON's mouth.

MADSON: Okay, we did it. The gun, the coke, the headaches, the stain. My knuckles, the amnesia, the epilepsy, and the girl in the trunk. We did it.

BARNUM: You did it.

COP: Open the trunk.

BARNUM: We have to get his tongue, gag him and give him his medicine. I can't help it if it's weird, he could die in there.

COP: Hand me the keys.

BARNUM: He's dying.

COP: Hand me the keys or I'll shoot you.

BARNUM hands the keys to COP.

COP covers the trunk with his gun, inserts the key and opens the trunk.

Thumping stops.

MADSON stops convulsing.

COP stares into the trunk…

Then closes the trunk and walks back to the driver's side window.

Get up.

BARNUM: Officer?

COP: Stop fucking around.

BARNUM: He's not breathing.

COP: Get up.

BARNUM: He's not breathing.

COP studies MADSON.

COP: I'll take his pulse.

COP takes MADSON's pulse.

I can't feel a pulse.

BARNUM: No pulse?

COP: Nothing.

BARNUM: Oh dude.

Pause.

So what's in the trunk?

Beat.

COP: Nothing.

Beat.

BARNUM: Oh my god man, I told you he could choke on his tongue.

COP: I thought you were lying.

BARNUM: Well, I guess you were wrong.

Beat.

You shouldn't be out here alone man, you're too new, it's irresponsible.

COP: I'm covering for my partner. He said it'd be alright.

BARNUM: Well it's not alright. You just killed my friend.

COP takes MADSON's pulse again.

COP: Maybe if we take him to a hospital…

BARNUM: No dude, you're fucked.

Beat.

COP: Oh.

Pause.

BARNUM: Come on man, what're you gonna do?

Beat.

COP: Well, I guess… I should call this in.

Beat.

BARNUM: Look, let's just put him in the trunk.

COP: What?

Beat.

BARNUM: Let's put him in the trunk.

COP: Why?

Beat.

BARNUM: Look man, I know how it is. You made a
    mistake, but I can tell you're a good cop.

Pause.

COP: Are you sure?

BARNUM: Yes.

Beat.

COP: Okay.

COP and BARNUM drag MADSON to the trunk.

They lift MADSON into the trunk and close it.

BARNUM: Okay.

COP: What are you going to do?

BARNUM: Let's not talk about it.

COP: Should we meet later?

BARNUM: No man. This is done. We should never meet or talk about it ever again.

Beat.

Okay?

COP: Okay, but let me ask you one thing and then we're done.

BARNUM: Sure.

COP: What happened to the girl?

Beat.

BARNUM: What girl?

COP: The girl in the trunk.

BARNUM: Did you see a girl in the trunk?

COP: No.

BARNUM: So there's no girl in the trunk.

COP: But is there a girl?

BARNUM: No man.

COP: Are you sure?

BARNUM: I swear to god.

Pause.

COP: Well, be careful.

COP turns to leave.

BARNUM: Hey, can I get my keys and stuff?

COP: Oh, sure.

COP hands BARNUM his car keys, then hands BARNUM his wallet, then holds out the motel key.

Is this yours?

Beat.

BARNUM: No.

COP pockets key.

Beat.

Crunching of gravel as COP walks away.

Okay, have a good night officer.

BARNUM gets into the driver's seat.

Pause.

BARNUM turns back toward the trunk...then looks to the road.

Black.

ACT TWO

Blackness. A motel room. The door opens. A black man (DEAN) enters, carrying a briefcase in one hand, and a white girl (STEPH), over his shoulder. She's handcuffed and gagged. She kicks and screams. He throws her on the bed, throws his keys on the bedside table, then turns the table lamp on.

DEAN: You comfy?

DEAN slides a pillow under her head.

STEPH whimpers through the gag.

Now let's just relax, get those shoes off you, you've been in those all day.

DEAN takes her shoes off.

STEPH tries to escape.

DEAN restrains her.

You're feisty aren't you? We're just going to fasten that down.

DEAN ties her cuffs to the bed frame with his belt.

He pulls antiseptic wipes from his briefcase.

He begins to clean STEPH.

Now look, let's get comfortable with each other here. We both want to have a nice time. I want to be nice to you. Just because you can't move or talk doesn't mean your hygiene has to suffer.

STEPH turns her head.

You're not looking at me. Look at me. Don't you remember me? I was the guy at the bar. Remember? I bought you that Fuzzy Navel, and now I'm looking at your navel. Hahaha…joking.

STEPH pleads through the gag.

I'm sorry what?

STEPH pleads through the gag.

I have no idea what you're saying. I find you really have to enunciate when you wear those things.

STEPH talks through the gag.

You like how I smell? I like how you smell. You have very pretty feet.

DEAN moves down to clean her foot.

STEPH whimpers through the gag.

DEAN's foot knocks glass.

He picks up a broken bottle.

What the fuck is this?

STEPH talks through the gag.

This place is a shithole. Someone could get a disease from this.

STEPH talks through the gag.

Whatever, no, it's fine it's fine.

DEAN disinfects hands with antiseptic wipes.

So, do you have any sisters?

Beat.

Don't like small talk, huh? Okay, well, I'm ready when you are.

STEPH talks through the gag.

Sounds like you're ready.

DEAN takes his shirt off, then mounts STEPH.

Three knocks on front door.

Beat.

STEPH talks through the gag.

Shh.

Three more knocks on front door.

Yea?

VOICE: Open the door.

DEAN: Who is it?

VOICE: It's the police.

Beat.

DEAN: What do you want?

VOICE: Open the door.

STEPH questions through the gag.

DEAN puts pillow over STEPH's face.

DEAN: You're sleeping.

VOICE: Open the door right now.

DEAN: Whoa man, alright.

DEAN walks to door and looks through peephole.

What do you want?

VOICE: Just open the door.

DEAN cracks door slightly.

DEAN: Sorry there officer sir, I was sleeping.

VOICE: Step outside.

DEAN: May I ask why?

VOICE: Just step outside.

DEAN: That's cool. Let me just get my shirt.

VOICE: Now.

DEAN: Oh I see, you're in a rush.

DEAN slides through the door and closes it behind him.

Outside motel room, COP guides DEAN to a wall. COP's hair is disheveled. He wears the pink purse. He holds the motel key. He pushes DEAN against the wall.

COP: What's your name?

DEAN: Do you need to push me sir?

COP: What's your name?

DEAN: Muhámmad.

Beat.

Dean.

COP: Muhammad Dean?

DEAN: Naw, that was a joke. Dean is my name.

COP: Dean what?

DEAN: Ali.

COP: Dean Ali?

DEAN: Kidding man, my last name's Brown.

COP: Dean Brown.

DEAN: That's right.

COP: Got identification?

DEAN: Yea, but not on me.

COP: Is this your room?

DEAN: Yea.

COP: Room number nine.

DEAN: That shit was just a joke, man, I'm not trying to give you a hard time.

COP: Don't cuss.

DEAN: Sorry.

COP: So that was a joke, you are not the occupant of this room?

DEAN: No I am.

COP: So it wasn't a joke?

DEAN: No well yes, that wasn't a joke, but before I was joking, about my name.

COP: Then what's your name?

DEAN: Dean.

COP: So what's the joke?

DEAN: I fucked up the timing of it.

COP: Don't cuss.

DEAN: Sorry.

Beat.

COP: Are you in there alone?

DEAN: Oh definitely.

COP: What are you doing here?

DEAN: Oh uh well I'm a law student, I'm on Spring Break, so, my buddies and I came to Vegas to kind of, and uh, well, to be honest sir my buddies told me about this place called the Bunny Ranch and uh, I'm a virgin and my buddies got together and paid for me to…you know…so…I was trying to find it, but I couldn't so I stopped here for the night.

COP: So what were you just doing?

DEAN: Oh just now? Sleeping like I said.

COP: Then why are you breathing heavy?

DEAN: Well I'm kind of embarrassed that I'm a virgin and about the uh, telling you about the Bunny Ranch because, not that I slept with any prostitutes because like I said I never found it but to tell you that, even though it's not illegal, is like – I don't know how you cops, officers, feel about all that…prostitution…it being legal and all? But anyway, it is legal right?

COP: So why are you sweating?

DEAN: That's from the hot shower I just took.

COP: You just said you were sleeping.

DEAN: I couldn't get to sleep so I took a shower to make me tired.

COP: So why are you sweating?

DEAN: The shower was hot and it's hot outside so that's two hot things, which made me sweat. That's not unusual, is it? I mean it's not illegal to breathe heavy or sweat is it? Hahaha, that was a joke.

COP: What's that on your arm?

DEAN: What?

COP: Is that blood?

DEAN: No man, lipstick.

COP: Lipstick?

DEAN: Alright I did find the Bunny Ranch, but uh, well, alright sir you got me.

COP: I thought you just took a shower.

DEAN: Right?

COP: Did you miss the lipstick?

DEAN: Oh. I left it on, you know, for fun. Like a memento, like when you visit the statue of liberty and buy a key chain…but uh, can I get my shirt on?

COP: You said you were hot.

DEAN: Ease up, the sweat cooled me down.

Beat.

This is all normal, why are you looking at me like that?

COP: Turn around.

DEAN: Just let me get my shirt on.

DEAN runs into motel room.

COP: Whoa, hold on Dean.

DEAN shuts the door, grabs his shirt, and searches for handcuff keys.

Open the door.

DEAN: I'll be right out.

COP opens door with motel key.

What are you doing?

DEAN blocks door.

You can't come in here.

COP: Back away Dean.

DEAN: You need a warrant.

COP: Back away or I'll shoot.

DEAN backs away.

DEAN: Alright alright calm down, this is against the law, but okay.

COP enters, gun drawn.

Beat.

COP: Who's that?

DEAN: Shh. Alright I brought the hooker back here.

COP: Get down Dean.

DEAN: I thought it was legal.

COP: Get down.

DEAN kneels.

DEAN: Okay, but keep your voice down.

COP: Ma'am, get up please.

DEAN: She's sleeping okay?

COP: Ma'am…

COP moves to bed.

DEAN: Leave her alone. You can't arrest her for prostitution because I haven't even paid her yet. I mean I will, if it's legal, and if it's not, then, you know, give me a break man I just got laid.

COP removes pillow and sees the gag.

DEAN stands.

That's uh, may look weird but she's definitely into it.

COP: Get down.

DEAN: Serious.

COP forces DEAN down.

COP: Hands behind your back.

DEAN: You're not gonna cuff me, are you?

COP: Hands behind your back.

DEAN puts his hands behind his back.

COP cuffs DEAN.

What are these scratches Dean?

DEAN: She got a little excited.

COP: Then why is she gagged?

DEAN: It's her gag. She gagged herself. She's self-gagged.

COP: Stay on the floor and shut up okay?

DEAN: Okay, okay, but she likes it.

COP: Now I told you to shut up.

DEAN: That's the truth.

COP: And I don't want to repeat myself.

DEAN: Serious.

COP: Fucking shut up.

Beat.

You're in serious trouble here Muhammad.

DEAN: Dean.

COP: I said shut up Mr Ali.

DEAN: Can I please just explain?

COP: Where are the keys?

DEAN: You don't have to yell.

COP pushes DEAN's head down.

COP: Where are the keys?

DEAN: In my pocket.

COP searches for the keys.

My right pocket.

COP extracts keys from DEAN's pocket.

Ow man.

COP: Again, no talking.

COP moves to the bed.

Don't be scared. I'm a police officer.

STEPH talks through the gag.

COP ungags STEPH.

Are you alright ma'am?

STEPH: Yea.

DEAN: Babe, you don't have to say anything.

COP: Are you hurt? Do we need to take you to the hospital?

STEPH: No.

DEAN: You don't have to listen to him.

COP: Shut up.

COP helps STEPH up and unlocks her cuffs.

Are you okay?

STEPH looks at DEAN.

STEPH: Yea.

COP: Don't look at him. Are you okay?

STEPH: Yes.

COP: You've been through a lot.

STEPH looks at DEAN.

STEPH: Okay, yea, I've been through a lot.

COP: What's your name sweetie?

STEPH: Steph.

COP: You're not a prostitute are you Steph?

STEPH: Sure.

COP: Oh you are a prostitute?

STEPH: Since I was twelve.

COP sits STEPH on edge of bed.

STEPH looks at DEAN.

COP: Alright, well it's okay that you're a prostitute. That's cool. What's important is that you're safe. I found you. The police are here. It's all over. Okay? Don't look at him.

STEPH smiles.

STEPH: Sorry.

COP: Now Steph I need to know if you remember anything about this evening.

DEAN motions to STEPH.

STEPH looks at DEAN.

Steph.

STEPH: What?

COP: Don't look at him. Do you remember anything about what happened to you?

STEPH: I don't know what you mean.

COP: Do you remember being in a car with two guys?

STEPH: Yes?

COP: You seem a little confused.

STEPH: I am confused sir.

COP: Probably a little disoriented, edgy – coke huh?

COP shows her a small plastic baggie.

STEPH: Oh yea, yea, lots of coke.

COP: Did you get coked up?

STEPH: Yes.

DEAN: What?

COP: It's alright, look, we're gonna find these guys.

DEAN: What are you talking about coke? That's not ours.

STEPH: Right, right, it's not our coke.

COP: Was this man in the car?

STEPH: Yes.

COP: Do you remember the other men?

DEAN: What the fuck are you doing?

COP: Wait, here – do you remember your purse?

COP shows her the pink purse.

DEAN: That's not hers.

COP: Shut up.

COP hands STEPH the pink purse.

I brought it for you.

STEPH: Thanks…

COP: You're welcome.

STEPH looks in purse.

Looking for the gun?

DEAN: Gun?

COP: I removed it of course.

DEAN: What the fuck are you talking about?

STEPH: Dean, what's going on?

DEAN: Steph, he's planting that shit on us.

COP stands.

COP: I told you not to talk.

STEPH: Wait a second.

COP takes out his nightstick.

DEAN: Fucking tell him Steph.

COP: But I'm obviously not making myself clear.

STEPH: Hold on officer.

COP puts nightstick in DEAN's mouth.

COP: Do you understand me better now?

STEPH pulls COP away from DEAN.

STEPH: Officer, officer, get off him. He's my boyfriend, you're making a big mistake.

COP shoves her back on the bed.

COP: Stay on the bed.

STEPH: He's my boyfriend, really, this is a big mistake.

COP: What?

STEPH: I'm not a hooker, he hasn't abducted me, I… I like it.

Beat.

COP: What are you saying?

Nightstick drops to floor.

DEAN: She's saying I'm her boyfriend, fuckpig.

COP: I do not appreciate that Dean. I do not appreciate you talking after I told you not to.

Pause.

So you were fucking with me?

STEPH: Sort of.

COP: Sort of? Goddamitt. Why the fuck are you fucking with me? I'm a fucking police officer. I could've fucking killed him. When I point a gun at you, you tell me the truth. You say, "yes sir" "no sir" and tell me what I want to hear.

STEPH: I thought I was telling you what you wanted to hear.

COP: Are you trying to tell me…that the two of you are doing some…dirty sex thing?

DEAN: Actually, we're hygiene obsessed.

Beat.

COP: What are you doing in this room?

STEPH: This is our room. We paid for it.

COP: So this isn't your purse?

STEPH: No.

COP: You said you did coke. Was that your coke?

STEPH: No.

COP: You're acting coked up.

DEAN: You're gonna arrest us for acting coked up?

Pause.

COP lays down on the bed.

Silence.

STEPH: Officer?

COP: Shh.

Pause.

COP sits up.

I'll be right back.

DEAN: Am I under arrest?

COP: Stay right where you are.

DEAN: You can't keep these cuffs on me.

COP: Don't move. Stay in here…lay down.

Beat.

DEAN slides to floor.

COP exits.

DEAN stands and looks through peephole.

DEAN: Oh my god Steph, what were you doing?

STEPH: What?

DEAN: You don't do that, you don't fuck with cops.

STEPH: Well you were fucking with him.

DEAN: I didn't accuse you of a felony.

STEPH: You told him I was a prostitute.

DEAN: Yeah but that's legal.

Beat.

STEPH: I thought he was part of it. I thought you like hired him.

DEAN: Why would I hire someone?

STEPH: It would've been hot I was into it.

DEAN: He cuffed me he was pointing a gun.

STEPH: I thought he was an actor it seemed so obvious.

DEAN: How?

STEPH: The purse the gun the cocaine.

DEAN: I might get arrested now.

STEPH: It seemed like a game.

DEAN: You don't fuck around with that. Do you know how hard it was for me to get into law school?

STEPH: I'm in college Dean. I know how hard it is.

DEAN: This is law school Steph, law, if I get arrested, I can't get my license, I can't be in school, they kick me out.

STEPH: Then why are you selling weed?

STEPH puts her shoes back on.

DEAN: I don't see how that's part of this conversation and please keep your voice down.

STEPH: Well I'm sure it will be fine, I mean we are innocent.

DEAN: Of what?

STEPH: Of whatever he suspects us of.

DEAN: How does that matter?

STEPH: You can't arrest someone if they're innocent.

DEAN: Do you know how easy it is for a cop to plant evidence?

STEPH: There are laws Dean.

DEAN: Not in buttfuck Nevada, this guy is probably his daughter's uncle.

STEPH: We'll get a lawyer.

DEAN: We'll get fucked.

One thump from bathroom.

Beat.

Did you hear that?

STEPH: What?

Beat.

DEAN: Really?

STEPH: What?

DEAN: Some noise.

STEPH: You're freaked out.

DEAN: No I heard a noise.

Beat.

STEPH: Hey, Dean.

DEAN: What?

STEPH: I'm getting all kinds of ideas.

DEAN: About what?

STEPH: About you and those handcuffs.

Pause.

Dean.

DEAN: Yea?

STEPH: It's gonna be okay.

Beat.

I can't believe they don't clean these rooms.

STEPH bends to pick up the broken beer bottle.

Ooh, it's got some nasty shit on it.

DEAN: What nasty shit?

STEPH: Dried crusty shit.

DEAN: We should hide it.

STEPH: I'll just toss it.

DEAN: Wipe my prints off of it.

STEPH: Dean, come on.

DEAN: Wipe it off with a towel from the bathroom.

STEPH: Jesus, Mr Freak Out.

STEPH moves toward the bathroom.

Door opens.

BARNUM enters.

BARNUM: Whoa, hey – stop.

STEPH: Who are you?

BARNUM: Who the fuck are you?

DEAN: Get the fuck out of our room man.

BARNUM: We're not renting out this room.

DEAN: Oh so then you work here?

BARNUM: I'm the night manager.

DEAN: Well I assure you we paid for the room.

BARNUM: No, there's a carbon monoxide leak in here.

STEPH: What?

BARNUM: Yea in the bathroom.

DEAN: There's a carbon monoxide leak?

BARNUM: Yea, you haven't been in there have you?

STEPH: No why?

BARNUM: For obvious reasons man.

Three thumps from bathroom.

DEAN: That's the fucking noise.

STEPH: That's coming from the bathroom.

BARNUM: Yea that's what I'm telling you we run a
generator in the basement and Carbon Monoxide is

coming up through the heating shaft – the air pressure is pushing against the vents – that's how we know we have a leak.

DEAN: What does that mean?

BARNUM: We'll have to fix it.

DEAN: For us?

BARNUM: You can asphyxiate man you shouldn't be in here.

STEPH: What should we do?

BARNUM: Cover your mouth.

STEPH covers her mouth.

DEAN: I can't cover my mouth.

STEPH covers DEAN's mouth with her hand.

BARNUM: I gotta check this out, breathe slowly until I get back.

BARNUM holds his breath, enters the bathroom and closes the door behind him.

Beat.

STEPH: Do you smell anything?

DEAN: Carbon Monoxide is odorless.

STEPH: Do you feel anything weird?

Beat.

DEAN: I don't know.

BARNUM comes out.

BARNUM: Oh man, it's worse than I thought. I gotta get you guys out of here.

DEAN: We can't leave.

BARNUM: What?

STEPH: We can't leave.

BARNUM: I can't understand you.

STEPH puts her hands down.

STEPH: The cop told us we had to stay.

BARNUM: Cops came in here?

DEAN: You didn't notice I was cuffed?

BARNUM: Well I thought it was some kinky shit.

STEPH: No, I wear the cuffs in the relationship.

Beat.

BARNUM: What did you guys do?

DEAN: Nothing.

BARNUM: Then why are you cuffed?

DEAN: He came in and started accusing us of shit.

BARNUM: Well you know cops around here.

STEPH: Not really.

BARNUM: Black dude, white chick…

DEAN: I fucking knew it.

STEPH: He thought I was somebody else.

DEAN: He tried to plant evidence on us.

BARNUM: Evidence?

DEAN: Yea, coke, a gun, this purse.

BARNUM: Whoa hold on I know this guy.

DEAN: You do?

BARNUM: Yea, you guys from out of state?

STEPH: Yea.

BARNUM: He's looking for a bribe.

DEAN: What do you mean?

BARNUM: He'll implicate you and tell you he's gonna take you in for questioning and if you don't pay him he'll arrest you.

STEPH: So what do we do?

BARNUM: Pay him.

STEPH: Bribe the cop?

BARNUM: Yea slip him some cash.

DEAN: Bribe a fucking police officer?

BARNUM: You never bribed a cop?

DEAN: No.

BARNUM: Oh man, you can get away with a lot of shit that way.

Beat.

DEAN: Well how do we do it?

BARNUM: Just give it to him.

STEPH: Just hand him the cash, don't we have to put it in an envelope or something?

BARNUM: Don't hand it to him slip it to him.

Beat.

DEAN: How much?

BARNUM: How much do you have?

DEAN: I can't reach my pocket.

STEPH searches DEAN's pocket.

STEPH: You've got like…three dollars, and thirty-two cents.

DEAN: Shit.

BARNUM: Well that won't be enough.

DEAN: How much do you have?

STEPH: Five.

DEAN: Fuck.

STEPH: How much do we need?

BARNUM: Come on guys you're gonna need at least a couple hundred.

DEAN: Do you think he'll take a MasterCard?

BARNUM: Absolutely.

DEAN: Really?

BARNUM: No dude.

Beat.

DEAN: So can we borrow some from you?

BARNUM: No man.

Beat.

BARNUM: What about those rings?

Beat.

STEPH: No way.

BARNUM: They're gold aren't they?

STEPH: Our promise rings?

BARNUM: That's like a couple hundred right there.

Beat.

DEAN: Alright.

STEPH: Dean.

DEAN: What?

STEPH: Our fucking promise rings.

DEAN: I'll buy you another one.

STEPH: Dean.

BARNUM: Come on come on get all that shit together.

STEPH hands DEAN her ring.

DEAN: Alright two rings, eight dollars and thirty-two cents.

STEPH: Only if we really need to.

DEAN: Is it gonna be enough?

One thump from bathroom.

BARNUM: Dude, do you guys feel that?

Beat.

DEAN: What?

BARNUM: Like a, headache?

Beat.

STEPH: No.

DEAN: Yea like a throbbing.

BARNUM: Whoa, I'm getting dizzy.

Beat.

Listen guys, I'm getting out of here.

DEAN: We can't leave.

BARNUM: Why not, it's not like he's actually got anything on you.

STEPH picks up DEAN's briefcase.

STEPH: Let's just go Dean.

BARNUM: I gotta lock this room up anyway.

DEAN: I'm handcuffed.

BARNUM: We'll saw them off.

DEAN: You got a hacksaw?

BARNUM: Of course.

DEAN and STEPH move to the door.

BARNUM picks up broken bottle.

Door opens.

Pause.

DEAN and STEPH back up as the COP ushers them back in.

Pause.

COP: Who's this guy?

BARNUM: Hello officer, I'm –

COP: I didn't ask you.

Beat.

COP: Do you all know each other?

STEPH: Yes.

DEAN: No.

BARNUM: We just met.

COP: Shh.

Beat.

Have a seat guys.

STEPH: Officer.

DEAN: Please.

COP: Have a seat.

BARNUM, DEAN and STEPH sit on the bed.

BARNUM stashes broken bottle.

So Steph, you know this man?

STEPH: Well sort of.

BARNUM: Officer I work here.

COP: Keep your hands out where I can see them.

BARNUM: Just let me explain why I'm here.

COP: I'm not asking you why you're here.

STEPH: Do you guys know each other?

BARNUM: There's a Carbon Monoxide leak in this room.

DEAN: And I got shooting pains in my eyes.

COP: Steph, what's this guy doing here?

STEPH: He's here to fix the leak.

Beat.

COP: You guys drink any alcohol tonight?

DEAN: We're sober sir.

COP: I said did you drink any alcohol?

STEPH: We had a few drinks.

DEAN: But not while we were driving.

COP: Nothing wrong with having a beer in your room.

COP takes out a white handkerchief.

DEAN: Officer I'm feeling light-headed.

COP: Well that's what happens when you drink.

DEAN: No because of the Carbon Monoxide.

COP: What do you got here – is this blood?

COP picks up the broken bottle with the handkerchief.

DEAN: What is that?

COP: Is this yours?

STEPH: Not at all sir.

COP: You just said you had a few beers.

DEAN: A few drinks.

STEPH: Not beers.

COP: So how did it get here?

STEPH: We don't know.

COP: Maybe it just rolled into your room.

DEAN: It was in the room when we got here.

COP: So you have seen this bottle before?

DEAN: Yes, when we first came in.

COP: Then why did you ask what it was?

DEAN: Because man, I'm not getting enough oxygen to my brain.

Beat.

COP: Alright guys, stand up, I'm gonna take you all into the station so we can ask you a few questions.

BARNUM nudges DEAN.

DEAN: What man?

COP: Get up.

BARNUM nudges DEAN.

DEAN: What?

COP: Come on get up.

DEAN stands.

DEAN: Oh officer.

COP: Steph, get up.

DEAN: Officer…uh…

COP: Take a deep breath Dean.

DEAN: The Carbon Monoxide is getting to me.

COP: Well, we're leaving right now.

DEAN: Right, about that…

DEAN drops the bills and change on the floor.

Beat.

COP: What is that?

DEAN: Aw man.

DEAN drops one of the rings.

COP: What is this Dean?

DEAN: Fine, here.

DEAN drops the other ring.

COP: Dean what are you doing?

DEAN: It's all I got man.

COP: Are you trying to bribe me with this?

Beat.

Bribing a police officer is a serious offense, Dean.

Beat.

DEAN: I got a hole in my pocket.

COP: You just committed a felony.

DEAN: No, I just accidentally dropped that.

COP: And I'm also pretty insulted.

DEAN: I'm sorry officer.

COP: Are those pennies?

DEAN turns to BARNUM.

DEAN: Now what?

BARNUM: I don't know.

COP: Did you tell him to bribe me?

BARNUM: Absolutely not, officer.

COP draws his gun.

COP: Everyone down on your knees.

STEPH gets down on her knees.

STEPH: We didn't do anything wrong.

DEAN: I think I have Carbon Monoxide poisoning.

COP: Get down Dean.

DEAN: I can't think.

COP: Get down.

COP forces DEAN down next to the bathroom door.

DEAN: Please don't put me by the door.

COP: Stay there.

DEAN: I feel so nauseous man.

COP: Barnum come here. Get down on your knees.

BARNUM: Are you gonna let this guy die too?

COP: Get on the floor.

COP throws BARNUM down.

DEAN: I can't breathe.

BARNUM: You're killing him man.

COP: Put your hands behind your back.

BARNUM: Just like you killed my friend.

STEPH: He can't breathe.

COP cuffs BARNUM.

BARNUM: Dude, I'm not gonna cover up your murder if you arrest me.

DEAN: I can't breathe I can't breathe.

COP: You're all under arrest.

BARNUM: No, you're under arrest.

STEPH: Officer please help Dean.

STEPH stands and moves to DEAN.

COP: Stay on the bed.

STEPH: Help him.

COP catches STEPH and holds both of her hands with his right hand.

BARNUM: You have the right to remain silent.

COP: You have the right to remain silent.

BARNUM: I just said that.

COP: Anything you say can and will be used against you in a court of law.

BARNUM: Ditto.

STEPH: Dean?

BARNUM: He's unconscious.

STEPH: Dean, answer me.

BARNUM: Help him.

STEPH: Please.

COP: Stop. Everyone shut the fuck up.

STEPH: Move him away from the door.

COP holsters his gun, pulls STEPH toward DEAN, then bends down to DEAN.

COP: Dean, can you hear me?

Pause.

One thump from bathroom.

COP looks up at the bathroom.

STEPH pulls out of COP's grasp and grabs the gun.

STEPH: Back away. Hands up. Hands up.

COP: Give me the gun.

BARNUM: Get the keys.

STEPH: Give me the keys.

COP: I want my gun back.

STEPH: Give me the keys right now.

COP gives STEPH the keys.

STEPH uncuffs DEAN.

COP: You don't want to do this Steph.

STEPH: Get up on the bed honey.

STEPH helps DEAN to the bed.

COP: I was helping him.

STEPH: Put your hands up.

COP: I was.

STEPH: Put your hands up.

STEPH tosses the cuffs to COP.

Cuff yourself.

COP cuffs himself.

COP: Okay, look, I'm willing to overlook this, I don't care what you guys did.

BARNUM: You're the only one breaking the law here.

STEPH: Get down on your knees.

COP: I just want to know where you're hiding the girl.

BARNUM: He's setting us up for something he did.

COP: I'm not.

DEAN: You're not going to fuck up my life.

COP: You made these choices, they're just coming back around.

DEAN: Well then you certainly have this coming.

DEAN picks up the nightstick.

Open.

DEAN puts nightstick in COP's mouth then steps back.

Pause.

BARNUM: Guys.

STEPH: Uh-huh?

DEAN: Yea?

BARNUM: We gotta get out of here.

DEAN: Right.

BARNUM: You can be tied to this room. Go to the front desk, talk to Jeff, tell him Chris sent you and to give you your paperwork. And tell him to give you my logbook. I'll erase your name.

Beat.

STEPH: And just leave?

DEAN: We gotta do something about...

BARNUM: Uncuff me. I'll watch him until you get back.

DEAN uncuffs BARNUM.

Alright, give me the gun.

COP protests through the nightstick.

STEPH: I'm not giving you the gun.

BARNUM: You wanna walk around outside with the cop's gun?

STEPH: Dean, take the gun, I'll go.

DEAN: I have to get out of here.

STEPH: I'm not staying in here.

DEAN: Alright, look, let's, let's, can we just give him the gun?

STEPH hands BARNUM gun.

DEAN moves behind COP.

So, I guess…we'll be right back.

BARNUM: Alright, man.

DEAN: And then we'll deal with the…

DEAN points to COP.

BARNUM: Yea.

DEAN and STEPH exit.

BARNUM walks to door and looks through peephole.

Isn't it interesting how anyone that came in here right now would probably think I was the bad guy? But that's just because you're wearing the uniform. You'd be in jail right now if it wasn't for me.

BARNUM takes nightstick out of COP's mouth.

But I don't think you're gonna have much of a future in law enforcement if you can't cover up a simple murder.

COP: Look, I'm sorry about your friend. I didn't mean for him to die.

BARNUM: Whatever, I'm living up to my side of the deal, I'm taking care of everything, but you're freaking out man.

COP: I don't think your friend was totally innocent.

BARNUM: Right, because of "the girl".

COP: There is a girl.

BARNUM: Yea, in your imagination.

COP: I know she exists. What did you do with her?

BARNUM: Sure, I understand, you killed a dude, you're in shock, you want to find someone to blame.

COP: Did you hurt her? If you did something to her…

BARNUM: What are you gonna do? Beat me with your stick or shoot me with your gun?

COP: I know you have her.

BARNUM: How?

COP: I just do.

BARNUM: Like you knew about the trunk?

Beat.

Two thumps from bathroom.

COP stands.

BARNUM chokes COP with nightstick.

Listen man, I'm innocent. I didn't do this, and I've never done any of this bad guy shit before. I just happen to be really good at it. Believe me, I'm as confused as you are. I'm a victim here, but it's good to know, I mean I've always wondered what I would do in a bad situation. Here it is, I mean…and I'm like surprising myself. My hands are steady, my mind is like ice, dude. I think I could be somebody.

COP falls unconscious on bed.

BARNUM picks up DEAN's keys from bedside table, turns

lamp off, and walks into bathroom.

BARNUM exits bathroom, dragging a body wrapped in a shower curtain. He lays the body down and opens the front door. Light spills into the room, reflecting off the shiny plastic of the shower curtain. BARNUM bends down, picks it up...

COP regains consciousness. BARNUM and COP stare at each other across the room. BARNUM drags body through door. Door shuts.

Black.

ACT THREE

Highway at night. Blackness. Tires hum on asphalt. Two headlights appear (DSC). Inside, three people occupy the car: the driver – DEAN, STEPH sitting shotgun, and BARNUM, in back between them, looking out the rear window.

DEAN: What the fuck are we doing?

BARNUM: Just go straight.

STEPH: Gun it Dean go.

DEAN: The pedal's on the floor.

BARNUM: Fucking calm down.

DEAN: You took my fucking keys.

BARNUM: I was waiting for you.

STEPH: Is that him?

 DEAN turns.

BARNUM: Keep your eyes on the road, man.

DEAN: Shut the fuck up.

STEPH: Dean watch out for the semi.

 DEAN swerves.

BARNUM: There's nobody behind us.

DEAN: You were not waiting for us.

BARNUM: You're in the car aren't you?

DEAN: Only because I threw myself on the fucking hood.

BARNUM: You were being paranoid man.

STEPH: Are those headlights?

DEAN: You stole our car.

BARNUM: The fucking cop attacked me. I had to get out. Trust me guys, I'm not trying to screw you here.

Beat.

Two thumps from trunk.

STEPH: What was that?

BARNUM: What?

STEPH: That.

BARNUM: What?

STEPH: That sound.

BARNUM: What the fuck are you talking about?

STEPH listens.

STEPH: Nothing.

Two thumps from trunk.

Dean? You don't hear that?

DEAN: I heard that.

STEPH: What did it sound like?

DEAN: Did we run over something?

BARNUM: What's going on?

STEPH turns around.

STEPH: I told you there's a sound.

BARNUM: I didn't hear anything.

DEAN: We both heard it.

Beat.

BARNUM: What are you looking at?

Beat.

One thump from trunk.

STEPH: There it is.

DEAN: I'm pulling over.

BARNUM: Don't pull over.

DEAN: It could be the car.

BARNUM: It's not the car.

STEPH: What is it?

BARNUM: It's those little bumpy reflector things they put down the centerline. Whoa guys whoa. Don't let the cops freak you out. Dean, you need to chill out and drive straight. Steph, you're paranoid. It's frightening. Fucking ease up. Jesus. Turn the radio on or something.

Two thumps from trunk.

Dean.

DEAN: I'm in my lane.

BARNUM: Turn the radio on.

STEPH: I don't think it's the road.

BARNUM: I'm telling you it's the road.

STEPH: Well I don't believe you.

Three thumps from trunk.

What the fuck what the fuck?

BARNUM: Stop freaking out.

DEAN: Don't yell at her.

STEPH: It's coming from the trunk.

BARNUM: Alright guys easy.

DEAN: I'm pulling over.

BARNUM: Don't stop.

DEAN: Why?

Two thumps from trunk.

STEPH: Why?

BARNUM: Look guys, you know the cop is crooked right?

STEPH: What's in the trunk?

BARNUM: And you know he's looking for a girl right?

STEPH: That girl with the purse?

DEAN: Why can't I pull over?

BARNUM: Well, she's in the trunk.

Pause.

DEAN: Why is she in our trunk?

BARNUM: She has to be in there man.

STEPH and DEAN exchange glances.

BARNUM: Guys, okay, I know what, you know, how this appears but –

DEAN: Well you can't, we can't, you know, this isn't, you know –

BARNUM: I'm not, I'm saying, I don't, I mean, she's okay –

STEPH: Oh really, in the trunk? Is it comfy? Does she like it in there?

BARNUM: She has to be in there, it's complicated, I know, I know –

DEAN: I'm pulling over, you're getting out, with this girl.

STEPH: Not with the girl.

DEAN: Yes with the girl.

STEPH: Dean.

BARNUM: No no guys, I'm helping her.

Beat.

STEPH: She must be thankful. That's why she's pounding on the trunk.

Two thumps from trunk.

BARNUM: She can hear you. She is thankful. Two thumps means she's okay. We're saving her life right now. Kathy, we'll get you out soon. Hold tight hon.

One thump from trunk.

DEAN: What does one thump mean?

BARNUM: It's good.

STEPH: Hello in there?

BARNUM: Don't bother her.

STEPH: Are you okay?

BARNUM: She's fucking scared.

DEAN: Of what?

BARNUM: Getting killed.

DEAN: Why?

BARNUM: She saw her boyfriend's murder.

DEAN: Why did he get murdered?

BARNUM: They drive cocaine into Vegas.

DEAN: Cocaine?

BARNUM: You know, for drug dealers.

STEPH: We know, Dean deals drugs.

DEAN: A little weed.

STEPH: Why did he get murdered?

BARNUM: He didn't pay the toll.

DEAN: What toll?

BARNUM: The toll to use the highway.

STEPH: Who collects the toll?

BARNUM: The cop.

Beat.

STEPH: Are those lights behind us?

Headlights silhouette the three. Twin beams reflect in DEAN's rearview mirror, casting a small horizontal rectangle across his eyes.

BARNUM looks through rear window.

BARNUM: Yes, someone's behind us.

STEPH: Is it the cop?

DEAN: Check the lights. Are they square?

BARNUM: They're pretty square.

STEPH: Are they cop headlights?

BARNUM: Yes, yes they are cop headlights.

DEAN: Fuck, it's him.

STEPH: He's following us?

BARNUM: Be calm. Drive normal. Maybe he doesn't know your car.

A siren begins: the horizontal bar flashes red and blue in DEAN's eyes.

DEAN: There go the lights.

STEPH: He knows it's us.

DEAN: How do you know all this?

BARNUM: Cut the lights.

DEAN: How do you know?

BARNUM: Cut the lights.

DEAN: I want to know how you're involved.

BARNUM: He was my friend.

STEPH: So you run drugs?

BARNUM: No I'm the night manager at a fucking motel. I'm trying to keep his girlfriend alive so cut the fucking lights.

DEAN cuts the lights.

STEPH: Can you see Dean?

DEAN: Not really.

BARNUM: Take this right.

DEAN: Where?

BARNUM: Up there

DEAN: Is that even a road?

BARNUM: Take it.

DEAN: You're an innocent friend?

BARNUM: Yes. Turn.

DEAN: Totally innocent?

BARNUM: Totally. Turn.

DEAN takes a right.

Headlights behind them disappear.

Siren fades away.

DEAN: Now what?

BARNUM: Take this left.

STEPH: Where are we?

DEAN takes a left.

DEAN: Where's the cop?

STEPH: He's gonna kill us.

BARNUM: I don't see him.

STEPH: We're gonna die.

DEAN: Now what?

BARNUM: Pull over.

DEAN pulls over.

STEPH: Does everyone agree? We're gonna die?

BARNUM: Calm down.

DEAN: Now what?

BARNUM: Cut the engine.

DEAN cuts the engine.

STEPH looks back toward the trunk.

STEPH: Dean.

DEAN: Steph.

STEPH: What do you think?

DEAN: We should run.

STEPH: We can't leave her.

DEAN: What if he finds us?

BARNUM: Don't worry, I've got it figured out.

DEAN: Oh yea? What would you do?

BARNUM: I'd get out.

DEAN: Then what would we do?

BARNUM: Well, he'd walk up.

DEAN: Yes I know, but what the fuck would we do?

BARNUM: Stall him.

DEAN: And what would you do?

BARNUM: I'd come up on him from behind.

   Beat.

DEAN: And do what?

   Beat.

   Headlights reappear behind them.

STEPH: Oh my god.

BARNUM: It's okay.

STEPH: Square headlights.

BARNUM: He doesn't see us.

STEPH: He's turning.

Headlights disappear.

DEAN: Where's he going?

STEPH: What's he doing?

DEAN: He's coming towards us.

Headlights hit the side of the car, angling up.

You fucked us man.

STEPH: He's gonna hit us.

BARNUM: You guys, shut up.

DEAN: He's stopping.

They stare (SR) into the headlights, which shine up at them through the car door windows.

BARNUM takes out the COP's gun and exits out the dark side (SL) of the car.

STEPH: No no no.

DEAN: You're staying here.

BARNUM: I'm gonna loop around.

STEPH: What are you going to do to the cop?

BARNUM: Don't worry.

STEPH: Don't kill him.

DEAN: What about the girl man?

BARNUM: What about her?

STEPH: What do we tell him?

BARNUM: Don't tell him anything.

DEAN: Where are you going?

BARNUM: Or he'll shoot you dude.

BARNUM exits (SL).

Pause.

STEPH: I feel awful Dean.

DEAN: I know I know it's sad about the girl.

STEPH: No Dean, I mean I feel really awful.

DEAN: Me too it sucks.

STEPH: No, I mean yes, it does suck, but that's why I feel awful because, because even though it's sad it's like, it's like…

Beat.

I feel excited.

Beat.

DEAN: That's adrenaline Steph.

STEPH: I know.

DEAN: That's normal.

Beat.

STEPH: Dean…

DEAN: Steph –

STEPH: Yea?

DEAN: Concentrate.

STEPH: Uh-huh.

DEAN: What do we want to do?

STEPH: Okay okay, well a killer cop has chased us down and, there's a fucking, someone's in our trunk.

DEAN: And we don't know who.

STEPH: Or what's up with her in there.

DEAN: Or exactly how she came to be in there.

STEPH: But she needs to get out.

DEAN: But not right now.

STEPH: What if she's hurt?

DEAN: What if she's dead?

STEPH: She's not dead, she's banging on the trunk.

DEAN: Not recently.

Beat.

STEPH: She should go to the hospital if she's hurt.

DEAN: Okay but if they catch us with her, we'll go to jail.

STEPH: Why?

DEAN: We don't know how things work around here, plus what we just did back there, plus our situation, my situation, who I am, you know?

STEPH: You mean because you're black?

DEAN: No. Yes, no. I guess more because of my job, my school, my life, what I've done so far, all this shit I've done to get here and you, obviously, and now because of this...thing I didn't even do...

STEPH: Are you suggesting we give her to the cop?

Beat.

DEAN: Well...

STEPH: Are you saying like sacrifice her for us?

DEAN: Well I mean she is a drug runner.

STEPH: Maybe.

DEAN: Maybe, and if so, she has it coming.

STEPH: You sell drugs.

DEAN: Weed, a little weed, to get through school, to improve my station in life.

STEPH: So you have it coming?

DEAN: In this situation, if she was me and I was in the trunk.

STEPH: Scared, possibly hurt, possibly suffocating, as we speak.

DEAN: Right. I would, I would, uh, I mean I would expect her to give me up.

STEPH: To be killed.

DEAN: Whatever, whatever situation I had gotten myself into.

STEPH: We will have killed her.

DEAN: She did it, she took that risk.

STEPH: She witnessed her boyfriend's death.

DEAN: Each person takes responsibility for their own situation.

STEPH: No Dean.

DEAN: Think about it.

STEPH: No.

Flashlight shines on them from behind.

COP: (*O.S.*) Get your hands out where I can see them.

DEAN: Officer...

STEPH: Dean.

COP: (*O.S.*) Get your hands up now.

COP enters (SR) at the rear of the car, flashlight in one hand, supporting the other, which holds the purse gun, which points at DEAN and STEPH.

DEAN and STEPH stare at each other.

Up, up, up where I can see them.

DEAN and STEPH raise their hands.

COP approaches the car slowly from behind.

DEAN: Officer…

STEPH: Dean.

COP: Shut up. Barnum, get up. I know you're in there. Get up.

STEPH: He's not in here.

COP: Where's my gun?

STEPH: Don't you have it in your hand?

COP: No, my gun, my gun, the one you fucking took.

STEPH: Oh, he took it with him.

COP: Barnum get up now.

DEAN: He's not here.

STEPH: Honestly.

DEAN: Don't shoot officer.

COP reaches the car and points the gun into the backseat.

Beat.

COP: Where is he?

DEAN: Not here.

COP ducks and shines the flashlight into the darkness.

COP: He was in there.

STEPH: No.

COP: He was in the car.

DEAN: Not in this car.

COP: I saw him.

DEAN: When?

COP: When you were resisting arrest, when you tried to outrun me, when you left the scene of a very bad crime.

STEPH: I didn't want to take your gun officer, you made me.

COP: Where is he?

COP shines flashlight back on DEAN and STEPH.

STEPH: We don't know.

COP: Where's the girl?

DEAN: What girl?

COP: The purse girl. The girl you all raped and tortured. Where is she?

DEAN: We have no idea what you're talking about.

STEPH: Why would I rape a girl, officer?

COP: That's fine. You're under arrest. Get out of the fucking car.

DEAN: You're arresting us?

STEPH: How can you do that officer?

DEAN: Didn't you kill a man?

STEPH: Aren't you guilty?

DEAN: Won't you be tried as well?

COP: Get out of the car.

COP rips STEPH out of the car and bends her over the hood.

You think you can stop me. I'm going to find the girl. I'm going to arrest those responsible. You are here. You were in there with him. I know you're involved.

COP rips DEAN out of the car and bends him over the hood.

I may lose this job. I may go to jail. But so will you. And before I turn you all in and give myself up, I'm finding the girl.

DEAN and STEPH look at each other.

DEAN: We were not involved in this officer, but Barnum was in the car.

STEPH: And the girl.

DEAN: She was in the car too but we dropped them off.

COP: Where?

DEAN: In the, in the, back there.

COP: In the desert?

DEAN: I guess.

COP: What was he going to do with her out there?

Pause.

STEPH: We don't know.

COP: So you killed her, he's burying her.

DEAN: He had your gun.

STEPH: He held us at gunpoint.

DEAN: He forced us to drive.

STEPH: He ordered Dean to lose you.

DEAN: And then he made us stop.

STEPH: And he dumped her out.

COP: So she's dead? She's definitely dead?

STEPH: We don't know.

COP: You all fucking killed her.

DEAN: He wouldn't let us look at her.

COP: Where is he? Where exactly?

STEPH: Back a ways.

COP: How far?

STEPH: Like half a mile back.

DEAN: You can probably still find him officer.

One thump from trunk.

Beat.

COP: So I could still get him?

STEPH: Yes, he's back by that turn.

COP: That last turn back there?

DEAN: Yea, the one with the sign.

COP: Okay you stay here.

COP steps back slowly.

DEAN: You're going?

COP: Yes, I'll be right back.

STEPH: What should we do?

COP: Stay here.

DEAN: Okay officer.

STEPH: We're sorry.

DEAN: We'll stay right here.

Beat.

COP points his gun at DEAN and STEPH and holds his finger to his lips as he walks back.

Pause.

Two thumps from trunk.

COP: He's in the trunk isn't he?

DEAN: No.

COP: He's fucking hiding in the trunk.

STEPH: No officer no.

COP moves back to trunk.

DEAN: Don't go back there officer.

COP: Barnum…

STEPH: It's a trap.

DEAN: He'll kill you.

COP: You put that girl in the trunk…

STEPH: He's waiting for you officer.

COP: And then you killed her…

DEAN: Don't.

STEPH: Please.

COP: And now you're in the trunk…

DEAN: He's got the gun.

STEPH: He'll shoot you.

COP: And there's a reason for that Barnum…

DEAN: Please step back officer.

COP: Because things come around….

STEPH: Stop. Stop. Stop.

> *Beat.*

> *COP fires into the trunk until the chamber clicks empty.*

> *Beat.*

COP: Pop the trunk.

STEPH: Officer.

COP: Pop the trunk.

> *Trunk pops open.*

> *COP lifts the trunk….*

> *Pause.*

> *Puts his hands to his head…*

> *Takes two steps back…*

> Fuck.

> *Takes two steps into the road…*

> *Doubles over, waiting to vomit…*

> Fuck.

DEAN: Officer.

COP: Fuck.

BARNUM enters with COP's gun.

BARNUM: Officer.

COP turns around…

Beat.

COP looks at his gun.

Beat.

BARNUM lifts the trunk.

Beat.

Now you're gonna let us go…

COP: You put her in the trunk?

BARNUM: Partly because we're innocent… But mostly because you just shot this fucking girl six times.

Pause.

COP: You put her in here.

BARNUM: Six times.

COP: You kidnapped her.

BARNUM: I'm innocent. I didn't do any of this. My friend told me he got in a fight with his girlfriend. They were fucked up. There was an accident. He asked for my help. We were gonna bring a doctor back to the room, but you pulled us over.

COP: Did you see her face?

BARNUM: After you shot her or before?

COP: There were gouges.

Beat.

That was no accident.

BARNUM: I didn't know that. I didn't know he had abducted her until you found that fucking gag. But I couldn't be honest with you. You wouldn't have cared. The only way to get out was to help you cover up your mistake. And I did. And look at this. Another mistake. And now we're gonna have to cover this one up too.

COP: If you're sure you're innocent why don't we just turn it in?

BARNUM: Because you're a cop.

COP: I'll admit what I've done.

BARNUM: You'll be protected. We'll go to jail.

COP: I'll be honest. I'll tell the truth.

Beat.

BARNUM: We gotta cover this up.

COP: I'm gonna call it in.

BARNUM: No you won't man.

COP: Or what, will you shoot me? And will you still be innocent then?

COP lays the purse in the trunk.

Pause.

COP walks away.

BARNUM: Are you walking away from this, man?

COP: I'm going to call it in.

BARNUM: Please, don't walk away from this.

Beat.

BARNUM follows him.

Don't walk away from this, man.

BARNUM exits.

Pause.

STEPH: Should we go?

DEAN: Not if he calls it in.

Beat.

STEPH: What do we do?

One gunshot.

Beat.

DEAN: Get in the car.

DEAN and STEPH get in the car.

BARNUM reappears.

BARNUM: Hold on guys.

DEAN: We're cool man.

BARNUM walks in front of the car.

BARNUM: Do not start the car.

STEPH: Don't kill us.

DEAN: Don't shoot.

Beat.

BARNUM: It's not like I…do this often, you know?

Beat.

I mean do you?

BARNUM walks to DEAN's window.

DEAN: What?

BARNUM: I mean you saw what happened. What he did. I'm not one of those, I'm not naturally like, uh, like one of those guys, who like, has fingers and heads in his freezer and doesn't even know it…

Beat.

I'm not, right?

STEPH: Yes.

DEAN: No.

STEPH: Don't kill us.

Beat.

BARNUM: Guys come on. I'm just like you. After all, you didn't exactly tell the cop the truth about what was in the trunk, did you? And you're not serial killers right?

Beat.

We have to think about this, decide what's right and what needs to be done. And when we all come to an agreement, then we'll do it. Okay?

Beat.

DEAN: Sure.

BARNUM: We need to keep all options open and that means you take the girl's body, okay?

Pause.

Because it can't be found. So can you do that?

Beat.

DEAN: Yes.

BARNUM: How about you?

STEPH: Yes.

BARNUM: Now you're gonna have to burn it or something.

DEAN: Burn it?

BARNUM: Can you do that without getting caught?

STEPH: Yes.

BARNUM: Okay. Because just let me know now if you can't.

DEAN: Oh we can do it.

BARNUM: Okay. So now later when we get our thoughts together we should talk. So I need your phone number.

Pause.

STEPH: You want our phone number?

BARNUM: To decide what to do, right?

DEAN: Right.

BARNUM: So what is it?

Beat.

DEAN: I can't remember.

Beat.

BARNUM: That's weird, your own phone number?

DEAN: Yea, uh, I'm blanking.

STEPH: I know it.

BARNUM: Do you have a piece of paper?

STEPH: All I've got is a pen.

BARNUM: Okay well, just write it on my hand.

DEAN: I just can't remember.

BARNUM offers STEPH his gun hand.

STEPH writes on BARNUM's hand.

BARNUM: I sort of feel like we're at a bar or something.

STEPH: There you go.

DEAN: Oh yea, that's it.

Beat.

BARNUM: Hey, can I have that pen?

STEPH hands him the pen.

BARNUM walks to the trunk.

BARNUM: I'm gonna get your license plate too.

Beat.

DEAN: Great.

Beat.

BARNUM returns pen.

What are you gonna do about the…?

BARNUM: Do you want to talk about it?

DEAN: I guess not.

Beat.

So I can count on you guys?

STEPH: Yes.

BARNUM: Okay. Be careful.

DEAN: Okay man.

BARNUM: I mean that.

Beat.

DEAN: Okay.

BARNUM exits.

Whoa.

STEPH: Yeah, Jesus.

Beat.

DEAN: Alright, let's go get some gas.

STEPH: Why, are we low?

DEAN: No.

Beat.

STEPH: Dean…

DEAN: Let's not talk about it, let's just do it.

STEPH: We can't just, you know… We…

DEAN: We didn't have a choice.

Pause.

Look, let's just go, okay?

STEPH: Fine.

DEAN: Fine.

Beat.

Do you hear that?

Beat.

STEPH: What?

DEAN: You don't hear that?

Three thumps from trunk.

Beat.

DEAN and STEPH look back at trunk.

Then turn back to face the road.

Two thumps from trunk.

Black.

End.